TikTok Cookbook 2023

Unleashing the Flavors of Viral Food Trends

Amy M. Garza

Copyright

Copyright © 2023 by Amy M. Garza

All rights reserved. No part of this book, "TikTok Cookbook 2023: Unleashing the Flavors of Viral Food Trends," may be reproduced, distributed, or transmitted in any form or by any means, including photocopying, recording, or other electronic or mechanical methods, without the prior written permission of the author, except in the case of brief quotations embodied in critical reviews and certain other noncommercial uses permitted by copyright law.

The recipes, text, images, and other content contained within this book are protected by copyright law and are the intellectual property of the author. Unauthorized reproduction, distribution, or transmission of any part of this book may result in legal action and claims for damages.

The author has made every effort to properly credit and acknowledge all sources, including TikTok creators and other reference materials, used in the creation of this book. Any unintentional omissions or errors are not intended to infringe upon the rights of others.

The content of this book is for personal use and enjoyment only. It is not to be resold, copied, or distributed for commercial purposes without the express written consent of the author.

For permissions, inquiries, or further information, please contact:

Amy M. Garza
echobuchobs@gmail.com

By purchasing, accessing, or using this book, you acknowledge and agree to abide by the copyright laws and the terms and conditions set forth in this copyright notice.

Thank you for respecting the hard work, creativity, and intellectual property of the author.

Amy M. Garza
Expert in the field of nutrition and digestive health.

Disclaimer Notice

The information and recipes presented in this book, "TikTok Cookbook 2023: Unleashing the Flavors of Viral Food Trends," are intended for educational and entertainment purposes only. While every effort has been made to ensure the accuracy and reliability of the content, the author and publisher make no representations or warranties of any kind, express or implied, about the completeness, accuracy, reliability, suitability, or availability with respect to the information, recipes, or related graphics contained in this book.

The recipes featured in this book have been inspired by viral food trends on TikTok and have been curated based on the author's personal interpretation. It is important to note that individual tastes, preferences, and dietary restrictions may vary. The author and publisher are not responsible for any adverse reactions, allergies, or health issues that may arise from the consumption or preparation of the recipes in this book. Readers are advised to exercise caution and seek professional advice if they have specific dietary concerns or health conditions.

Furthermore, the author and publisher do not endorse or guarantee the success of any TikTok food challenges, collaborations, or trends mentioned in this book. Participation in such activities is at the reader's discretion and should be undertaken with proper care and consideration.

The author and publisher disclaim any liability for loss, injury, or damages arising from the use or reliance upon any information or recipes presented in this book. The reader assumes full responsibility for any actions taken based on the content of this book.

It is recommended that readers follow proper food safety guidelines, including but not limited to proper handling, cooking, and storage of ingredients. Readers should also exercise caution when using kitchen tools and equipment, following manufacturer instructions and practicing necessary safety precautions.

Please note that the TikTok platform is dynamic, and trends may change over time. While efforts have been made to ensure the relevance and accuracy of the content at the time of publication, the author and publisher cannot guarantee that the recipes and information will remain current or reflective of ongoing TikTok trends.

By using this book and its recipes, readers acknowledge and agree to the above disclaimer, understanding that they assume full responsibility for their actions and any consequences that may arise from the use of the information and recipes provided.

Amy M. Garza
Expert in the field of nutrition and digestive health.

Table of Contents

Copyright
Disclaimer Notice
Table of Contents
Forward
About The Book
Reader's Guide
Introduction
Chapter 1: Getting Started with TikTok Cooking
Chapter 2: Breakfast and Brunch Delights
Chapter 3: Lunch and Snack Sensations
Chapter 4: Dinner Winners
Chapter 5: Desserts that Delight
Chapter 6: TikTok Food Challenges and Collaborations
Chapter 7: Navigating Food Trends on TikTok
Chapter 8: Personalizing and Putting Your Spin on TikTok Recipes
Chapter 9: Embracing TikTok Cooking as a Culinary Adventure
Conclusion: Embracing TikTok Cooking as a Culinary Adventure
About The Author
Appendix: Essential TikTok Recipes Index
Glossary of TikTok Cooking Terms
Gift/ Bonus!
Acknowledgments

Forward

When it comes to the world of culinary exploration, TikTok has emerged as a captivating platform that has revolutionized the way we discover, create, and share recipes. With its short, snappy videos and an enthusiastic community of food enthusiasts, TikTok has become a hub of viral food trends that captivate our taste buds and inspire our creativity in the kitchen.

I am thrilled to write the foreword for "TikTok Cookbook 2023: Unleashing the Flavors of Viral Food Trends," a remarkable book that takes readers on a flavorful journey through the exciting world of TikTok cooking. This book, authored by [Your Name], is an exceptional guide that captures the essence of TikTok's culinary culture and brings it to life through an array of delectable recipes.

In "TikTok Cookbook 2023," Amy presents an impressive collection of TikTok-inspired recipes that showcase the diversity, creativity, and innovation found on the platform. From fluffy pancakes and mouth watering pasta dishes to tantalizing desserts and refreshing smoothie bowls, this book caters to a wide range of tastes and preferences, ensuring that there is something for everyone.

What sets this book apart is [Your Name]'s deep understanding of the TikTok community and the ability to curate recipes that not only taste amazing but also reflect the spirit of TikTok cooking. The recipes are carefully crafted, with clear instructions and informative cook's tips that empower readers to recreate the dishes with confidence.

Moreover, Amy understands the importance of personalization and encourages readers to adapt the recipes to their own tastes and dietary needs. This book serves as a valuable resource for both novice and experienced home cooks, providing them with the tools and inspiration to unleash their creativity in the kitchen.

Throughout the pages of "TikTok Cookbook 2023," Amy takes us on a culinary adventure, sharing stories of the viral food trends that have captivated TikTok users worldwide. The book goes beyond the recipes themselves, delving into the influence of TikTok on culinary trends, exploring popular food challenges, and providing insights on how to stay ahead of the curve.

As you embark on this culinary journey, I encourage you to embrace the joy of cooking, to experiment with flavors, and to connect with the vibrant TikTok culinary community. Let "TikTok Cookbook 2023" be your guide, opening up a world of flavors, techniques, and possibilities that will elevate your cooking skills and ignite your passion for culinary exploration.

I commend Amy for her dedication, expertise, and passion in bringing the flavors of TikTok to our kitchens through this extraordinary book. It is a testament to their love for food, their commitment to sharing knowledge, and their desire to inspire others to discover the delights of TikTok cooking.

So, grab your apron, sharpen your knives, and get ready to unleash the flavors of viral food trends with "TikTok Cookbook 2023." May this book serve as your companion, guiding you through an exciting culinary adventure that will leave you inspired, satisfied, and eager to share your creations with friends and family.

Kurt E. Malloy, PhD
Gastroenterologist and Acid Reflux Researcher

About The Book

Amy M. Garza
Expert in the field of nutrition and digestive health.
June, 2023.

"TikTok Cookbook 2023: Unleashing the Flavors of Viral Food Trends"

I am pleased to provide a reference for the book "TikTok Cookbook 2023: Unleashing the Flavors of Viral Food Trends," authored by Amy M. Garza. This book is a comprehensive and engaging guide that explores the world of TikTok cooking and showcases a collection of captivating and delicious recipes inspired by viral food trends.

"TikTok Cookbook 2023" is a well-researched and meticulously curated compilation of TikTok recipes that reflect the dynamic nature of the platform's culinary landscape. The book takes readers on a culinary adventure, introducing them to a variety of TikTok-inspired dishes, from breakfast delights and lunch sensations to dinner winners and mouth watering desserts.

The author demonstrates a deep understanding of TikTok's food culture, highlighting the influence of viral food videos and exploring the power of TikTok in shaping culinary trends. Through clear and concise instructions, the book empowers readers to recreate these viral recipes in their own kitchens, providing essential tools, ingredients, cooking techniques, and cook tips to ensure success.

What sets "TikTok Cookbook 2023" apart is the author's ability to capture the essence of TikTok cooking while infusing a personal touch. The recipes are not only delicious but also versatile, allowing readers to adapt them to their own tastes and dietary needs. The book encourages creativity, inspiring readers to put their own spin on the TikTok recipes and providing guidance on how to add their creative touch to TikTok food videos.

Moreover, the author's exploration of TikTok food challenges and collaborations adds an exciting element to the book, encouraging readers to participate and engage with the TikTok culinary community. The book also delves into the identification and anticipation of food trends on TikTok, providing readers with valuable insights to stay ahead of the curve.

Throughout the book, the author's passion for food and commitment to sharing knowledge shine through.

The recipes are accompanied by beautiful visuals, enhancing the reader's experience and making the dishes even more enticing. The inclusion of nutritional information for each recipe is also commendable, enabling readers to make informed choices about their dietary preferences.

I highly recommend "TikTok Cookbook 2023: Unleashing the Flavors of Viral Food Trends" to anyone interested in exploring the world of TikTok cooking, discovering new flavors, and embracing culinary creativity. This book not only offers a wealth of delicious recipes but also serves as a guide to navigating the TikTok food culture and becoming an active participant in this exciting community.

Amy M. Garza
Expert in the field of nutrition and digestive health.

Reader's Guide

"TikTok Cookbook 2023: Unleashing the Flavors of Viral Food Trends"

Welcome to "TikTok Cookbook 2023: Unleashing the Flavors of Viral Food Trends." This reader's guide is designed to help you navigate through the book and make the most of your culinary journey into the world of TikTok cooking. Here's what you can expect and how to use this guide effectively:

1. Introduction:
   - Start by reading the introduction, which sets the stage for the book and provides an overview of the rise of TikTok food culture. Gain insights into the influence of TikTok on culinary trends and understand the power of viral food videos.

2. Chapters:
   - The book is divided into several chapters, each focusing on a specific category of recipes. Dive into the chapters that pique your interest or explore them all to discover a wide range of delicious TikTok-inspired dishes.

3. Recipe Format:
   - Each recipe is presented in a standardized format for ease of understanding. Pay attention to the list of ingredients, cooking instructions, cook tips, and nutritional value provided. This information will help you prepare the recipes with confidence and make informed choices about your dietary preferences.

4. Cook's Tips:
   - Throughout the book, you will find valuable cook's tips and insights shared by the author. These tips are designed to enhance your cooking skills, provide alternatives or variations, and offer suggestions for personalizing the recipes.

5. Appendix: Essential TikTok Recipes Index:
   - The appendix contains an index of essential TikTok recipes featured in the book. Use this index as a quick reference guide to locate your favorite recipes or revisit the ones you have tried and loved.

6. Glossary of TikTok Cooking Terms:
   - Flip to the glossary section to familiarize yourself with common TikTok cooking terms. This will help you understand the language and terminology used in the TikTok culinary community.

7. Acknowledgments:
- Don't forget to read the acknowledgments section to appreciate the individuals who contributed to the creation of this book. It's a great way to recognize the efforts of the author, the TikTok community, and the team involved in bringing this book to life.

8. Reference:
- Finally, the reference section provides additional information and resources for further exploration of TikTok cooking or related topics.

Remember, this book is meant to be a guide and a source of inspiration. Feel free to adapt the recipes to suit your personal taste preferences, dietary restrictions, or ingredient availability. Embrace your creativity and put your own spin on the TikTok recipes you discover within these pages.

Enjoy the flavors, the excitement, and the joy of cooking as you delve into the world of TikTok culinary trends. Happy cooking and bon appétit!

Amy M. Garza
Expert in the field of nutrition and digestive health.

Introduction

The world of social media has revolutionized various aspects of our lives, and one area where its impact is particularly prominent is in the realm of food culture. With the advent of platforms like TikTok, the culinary landscape has witnessed a significant transformation. This article delves into the rise of TikTok food culture, exploring its influence on culinary trends and understanding the power of viral food videos.

1. The Rise of TikTok Food Culture

In recent years, TikTok has emerged as a cultural phenomenon, captivating millions of users worldwide with its short-form videos. While initially known for its dance challenges and lip-syncing videos, the platform has increasingly become a hub for food-related content. Food creators, both amateur and professional, have flocked to TikTok, showcasing their culinary skills and creativity in innovative and engaging ways.

1.1 Exploring the Influence of TikTok on Culinary Trends

TikTok's impact on culinary trends cannot be overstated. The platform has democratized food culture, allowing anyone with a smartphone and a passion for cooking to share their recipes, techniques, and food hacks with a global audience. This democratization has resulted in a diverse and dynamic culinary community where traditional and avant-garde recipes coexist.

One of the significant aspects of TikTok's influence on culinary trends is its ability to make cooking accessible and enjoyable. The short video format, often accompanied by catchy music or voice overs, breaks down complex recipes into easily digestible steps. This approach has inspired many people, including those who were previously intimidated by cooking, to venture into their kitchens and try their hand at new dishes.

Moreover, TikTok has sparked a renewed interest in home cooking and experimentation. Users are not only replicating popular recipes but also putting their unique twists on them. The platform's algorithm, which tailors content based on individual preferences, ensures that users are constantly exposed to fresh and exciting culinary ideas. This exposure fuels creativity and encourages users to push the boundaries of traditional cooking, resulting in an explosion of innovative recipes and flavor combinations.

1.2 Understanding the Power of Viral Food Videos

One of the driving forces behind TikTok's influence on food culture is the power of viral food videos. TikTok's algorithm thrives on trends, and when a food video goes viral, it spreads like wildfire across the platform. These videos often feature visually appealing dishes, creative presentation techniques, or unexpected flavor combinations that capture the attention and curiosity of viewers.

The virality of food videos on TikTok has several implications. Firstly, it has the potential to turn previously unknown dishes or ingredients into overnight sensations. A simple yet mesmerizing video of a unique food preparation technique or an aesthetically pleasing dish can generate a massive surge in demand for specific ingredients or cooking methods. This phenomenon has led to the rise of "TikTok food trends," where certain recipes or food products gain widespread popularity and become a part of popular culture.

Secondly, the virality of food videos has empowered small businesses and local eateries. By showcasing their culinary creations on TikTok, these establishments can reach a massive audience and garner attention that was previously reserved for larger, more established brands. This exposure often translates into increased foot traffic, online orders, and brand recognition, providing a much-needed boost to these businesses.

Furthermore, the power of viral food videos extends beyond the realm of food itself. TikTok's algorithm has a ripple effect, influencing other social media platforms and even traditional media outlets. Popular food videos often find their way onto Instagram, YouTube, and television programs, amplifying their reach and impact. This cross-platform promotion further cements TikTok's role as a trendsetter in the culinary world.

TikTok has ushered in a new era of food culture, revolutionizing how we discover, consume, and engage with culinary content. Its influence on culinary trends cannot be underestimated, as it has democratized cooking, made it accessible to a wider audience, and inspired creativity and experimentation in the kitchen.

Through its short-form videos, TikTok has broken down barriers and made cooking enjoyable and approachable for people of all skill levels. By presenting recipes in bite-sized steps, accompanied by music and engaging visuals, the platform has made cooking less daunting and more inviting. This has encouraged individuals who were previously hesitant to venture into the kitchen to try their hand at cooking, leading to an increase in home-cooked meals and a deeper appreciation for the culinary arts.

The platform's algorithm plays a crucial role in shaping culinary trends. By tailoring content to individual preferences, TikTok ensures that users are exposed to a diverse range of recipes and cooking techniques. This exposure fosters creativity and pushes users to experiment with different flavors, ingredients, and presentation styles. As a result, the TikTok food culture is marked by an abundance of innovative recipes, fusion cuisines, and unique culinary experiences.

The power of viral food videos on TikTok cannot be overstated. When a food video goes viral, it has the potential to transform obscure dishes or ingredients into sensations. The captivating visuals, unexpected combinations, and creative presentation techniques featured in these videos capture the attention and curiosity of viewers, leading to an increased demand for specific foods. This phenomenon has given rise to trends such as whipped coffee, cloud bread, and pancake cereal, which have gained immense popularity and become cultural phenomena.

In addition to the impact on individual users, viral food videos on TikTok have also proven beneficial for small businesses and local eateries. By showcasing their culinary creations on the platform, these establishments can gain exposure to a vast audience that was previously inaccessible. This exposure translates into increased foot traffic, online orders, and brand recognition, helping these businesses thrive in a competitive market.

The influence of TikTok's food culture extends beyond the platform itself. Popular food videos often find their way onto other social media platforms, where they are shared, reposted, and emulated. Instagram, YouTube, and even traditional media outlets frequently feature content that originated on TikTok. This cross-platform promotion amplifies the reach and impact of TikTok's culinary trends, solidifying the platform's status as a trendsetter in the food industry.

In conclusion, TikTok has revolutionized food culture by empowering individuals to explore their culinary passions, discover new recipes, and experiment in the kitchen. Its influence on culinary trends is profound, as it has made cooking accessible, inspired creativity, and propelled viral food videos to new heights. Whether it's the rise of unique food trends or the exposure it provides to small businesses, TikTok's impact on food culture is undeniable, shaping the way we eat, cook, and engage with the culinary world.

Chapter 1: Getting Started with TikTok Cooking

In recent years, TikTok has become a powerhouse platform for culinary enthusiasts to showcase their skills, share recipes, and inspire others with mouthwatering dishes. If you're eager to dive into the world of TikTok cooking and unleash the flavors of viral food trends, this chapter will guide you through the essential steps to get started. From setting up your TikTok cooking space to mastering the techniques that make TikTok recipes stand out, you'll be well-equipped to embark on your culinary journey.

1.1 Setting Up Your TikTok Cooking Space

Creating an inviting and functional space for your TikTok cooking adventures is essential. Consider the following aspects when setting up your TikTok cooking space:

1. Define your backdrop: Choose an area in your kitchen or home with good lighting and an appealing background. Natural light is ideal, but if that's not possible, invest in quality lighting equipment to ensure your videos are well-lit and visually pleasing.

2. Organize your cooking tools: Arrange your cooking tools in an orderly and easily accessible manner. Invest in open shelving or storage solutions to keep your utensils, pots, and pans within reach. A well-organized space will not only make your cooking process smoother but also enhance the visual appeal of your videos.

3. Personalize your space: Add your own unique touches to the cooking space to reflect your personality and style. Consider incorporating plants, artwork, or decorative elements that make the space visually appealing and inviting for your viewers.

4. Consider your camera angle: Experiment with different camera angles to find the one that works best for your cooking style. Ideally, your camera should capture the entire cooking process without obstructing any crucial steps.

1.2 Essential Tools and Ingredients for TikTok Recipes

To create TikTok-worthy recipes, it's essential to have the right tools and ingredients at your disposal. Here are some essentials you'll need:

1. High-quality camera: Invest in a smartphone or camera with good video quality to capture your cooking process. TikTok's short-form videos thrive on visually appealing content, so having a reliable camera is crucial.

2. Tripod or stabilizer: To ensure steady footage, consider using a tripod or stabilizer to hold your camera while you're cooking. This will help eliminate shakiness and produce professional-looking videos.

3. Mixing bowls and utensils: A set of mixing bowls in various sizes and a range of utensils like spatulas, whisks, and spoons will come in handy for different recipe preparations.

4. Non-stick pans and pots: Non-stick pans and pots are essential for cooking on TikTok. They facilitate easy food release and make for effortless cleaning.

5. Knife set: Invest in a good-quality knife set that includes a chef's knife, paring knife, and serrated knife. These will cover the majority of your cutting and chopping needs.

6. Cutting boards: Choose cutting boards that are durable and easy to clean. Consider having separate boards for meat, poultry, fish, and vegetables to prevent cross-contamination.

7. Essential ingredients: Stock up on staple ingredients used in popular TikTok recipes, such as flour, sugar, baking powder, salt, various spices, oils, vinegars, and soy sauce. Additionally, keep a selection of fresh produce and proteins on hand to experiment with different flavors and combinations.

1.3 Mastering TikTok Cooking Techniques

While TikTok recipes are known for their visually appealing presentation, they also rely on specific cooking techniques to create stunning dishes. Here are some techniques to master for TikTok cooking:

1. Plating and presentation: TikTok cooking emphasizes visually striking dishes, so take the time to plate your creations with care. Consider using garnishes, colorful ingredients, and unique serving vessels to enhance the presentation of your dishes. Experiment with different plating styles and techniques to make your recipes stand out on TikTok.

2. Speed and efficiency: TikTok videos have a limited time frame, so it's crucial to develop efficient cooking techniques. Practice chopping, slicing, and prepping ingredients quickly and confidently. Look for time-saving tips and tricks to streamline your cooking process without compromising on flavor.

3. Visual effects and transitions: TikTok is known for its creative visual effects and seamless transitions between different cooking stages. Explore the built-in video editing tools on the platform or use external video editing software to enhance the visual appeal of your videos. Incorporate captivating transitions and effects to engage your viewers and make your cooking content more captivating.

4. One-pot meals and one-pan wonders: TikTok recipes often emphasize simplicity and convenience. Explore one-pot meals and one-pan wonders that showcase a complete and flavorful dish cooked in a single vessel. These recipes not only save time but also make for visually appealing videos that highlight the beautiful combination of ingredients.

5. Innovative flavor combinations: TikTok cooking encourages experimentation with unique and unexpected flavor combinations. Don't be afraid to think outside the box and incorporate unconventional ingredients or spices into your recipes. Take inspiration from viral food trends and challenge yourself to create flavor profiles that surprise and delight your viewers.

6. Text overlays and captions: Text overlays and captions are essential elements in TikTok cooking videos. Use them to provide clear instructions, highlight key steps, or share tips and tricks with your audience. Keep the text concise, legible, and visually appealing to enhance the viewer's experience.

7. Engaging storytelling: TikTok is not just about sharing recipes; it's also an opportunity to connect with your audience on a personal level. Develop your storytelling skills by adding engaging and relatable narratives to your videos. Share anecdotes, cooking tips, or personal

experiences that resonate with your viewers, making them feel connected and inspired by your content.

By mastering these TikTok cooking techniques, you'll be able to create captivating and delicious recipes that captivate your audience and drive engagement on the platform.

This chapter introduces you to the world of TikTok cooking. By setting up your TikTok cooking space, equipping yourself with essential tools and ingredients, and mastering TikTok cooking techniques, you'll be ready to embark on a culinary journey filled with creativity, inspiration, and mouthwatering recipes. As you continue reading the book, you'll explore a wide range of viral food trends, learn exciting recipes, and uncover the secrets to creating TikTok-worthy dishes that leave a lasting impression. So, get ready to unleash your culinary prowess and become a TikTok cooking sensation!

Chapter 2: Breakfast and Brunch Delights

2.1 Fluffy Pancakes in TikTok Style

Ingredients:
- 1 ½ cups all-purpose flour
- 3 ½ teaspoons baking powder
- 1 tablespoon sugar
- ¼ teaspoon salt
- 1 ¼ cups milk
- 1 egg
- 3 tablespoons melted butter
- 1 teaspoon vanilla extract
- Optional toppings: fresh berries, maple syrup, powdered sugar

Cooking Instructions:
1. In a large bowl, whisk together the flour, baking powder, sugar, and salt.
2. In a separate bowl, whisk together the milk, egg, melted butter, and vanilla extract until well combined.
3. Pour the wet ingredients into the dry ingredients and gently whisk until just combined. Be careful not to overmix; a few lumps are okay.
4. Preheat a non-stick skillet or griddle over medium heat.
5. Using a ¼ cup measuring cup, pour the batter onto the skillet to form pancakes.
6. Cook the pancakes for about 2-3 minutes until bubbles start to form on the surface. Flip the pancakes and cook for an additional 1-2 minutes until golden brown.
7. Remove the pancakes from the skillet and repeat the process with the remaining batter.
8. Serve the fluffy pancakes warm with your choice of toppings such as fresh berries, maple syrup, or a dusting of powdered sugar.

Cooking Tips:
- For extra fluffy pancakes, separate the egg yolk and white. Beat the egg white until stiff peaks form, and then fold it into the batter gently before cooking.
- To keep the pancakes warm while cooking the rest, place them on a baking sheet in a preheated oven at 200°F (93°C) until ready to serve.

Nutritional Value (per serving):
- Calories: 250
- Carbohydrates: 35g
- Protein: 6g

- Fat: 9g
- Fiber: 1g

2.2 Creative Toast Creations for an Energizing Start

Ingredients:
- Slices of your preferred bread (whole wheat, sourdough, or gluten-free)
- Assorted toppings: avocado, sliced tomatoes, smoked salmon, cream cheese, fresh herbs, fried eggs, bacon, microgreens, etc.

Cooking Instructions:
1. Toast the bread slices in a toaster or under the broiler until golden brown and crisp.
2. Once toasted, let the bread cool slightly before adding the toppings.
3. Get creative with your toast creations! Here are a few ideas to inspire you:
    - Avocado Toast: Mash ripe avocado onto the toast, sprinkle with a pinch of salt and pepper, and top with sliced tomatoes and a drizzle of olive oil.
    - Smoked Salmon Toast: Spread cream cheese onto the toast, top with smoked salmon slices, thinly sliced red onions, and fresh dill.
    - Fried Egg Toast: Fry an egg to your liking (sunny-side-up, over-easy, or poached) and place it on the toast. Add salt, pepper, and your choice of herbs for extra flavor.
    - BLT Toast: Spread mayonnaise or aioli on the toast, layer crispy bacon, lettuce, and tomato slices. Season with salt and pepper.
4. Feel free to mix and match the toppings based on your preferences. Get creative and experiment with different flavor combinations.

Cooking Tips:
- For added flavor, drizzle the toast with balsamic glaze, hot sauce, or your favorite dressing.
- Don't limit yourself to savory toppings. You can also try sweet variations like nut butter with sliced bananas and a sprinkle of cinnamon or cream cheese with fresh berries and a drizzle of honey.

Nutritional Value (per serving):
The nutritional value will vary depending on the choice of bread and toppings. Here is an approximate range for the basic avocado toast recipe:
- Calories: 200-250
- Carbohydrates: 20-25g
- Protein: 5-8g
- Fat: 12-15g
- Fiber: 4-6g

2.3 Trendy Smoothie Bowls to Boost Your Morning

Ingredients:
- 1 frozen banana
- 1 cup frozen berries (such as strawberries, blueberries, or mixed berries)
- ½ cup milk (dairy or plant-based)
- 1 tablespoon honey or maple syrup (optional, for added sweetness)
- Toppings: sliced fresh fruits, granola, chia seeds, coconut flakes, nuts, edible flowers, etc.

Cooking Instructions:
1. In a blender, combine the frozen banana, frozen berries, milk, and honey or maple syrup (if desired).
2. Blend on high speed until smooth and creamy. If the mixture is too thick, add a splash of additional milk and blend again until the desired consistency is reached.
3. Pour the smoothie into a bowl.
4. Top the smoothie bowl with your choice of toppings, such as sliced fresh fruits, granola, chia seeds, coconut flakes, nuts, or edible flowers. Get creative and arrange the toppings in an aesthetically pleasing manner.
5. Serve the smoothie bowl immediately and enjoy it with a spoon.

Cooking Tips:
- To achieve a thicker consistency, use less liquid or add additional frozen fruits.
- Experiment with different flavor combinations by adding ingredients like spinach, kale, nut butter, or protein powder to customize your smoothie bowl.
- For an extra refreshing touch, add a squeeze of fresh lemon or lime juice to the smoothie mixture.

Nutritional Value (per serving):
The nutritional value of the smoothie bowl will vary depending on the choice of ingredients and toppings. Here is an approximate range for a basic smoothie bowl made with a frozen banana, mixed berries, and milk, topped with sliced fresh fruits and granola:
- Calories: 300-400
- Carbohydrates: 60-70g
- Protein: 6-10g
- Fat: 4-8g
- Fiber: 8-12g

Chapter 2 of the "TikTok Cookbook 2023: Unleashing the Flavors of Viral Food Trends" introduces you to an array of delightful breakfast and brunch options that have taken the TikTok world by storm. From fluffy pancakes to creative toast creations and trendy smoothie bowls, these recipes are designed to kickstart your day with flavors and presentations that are sure to impress. Whether you're craving a comforting stack of pancakes, a savory and visually appealing toast, or a refreshing and nutritious smoothie bowl, this chapter has you covered. So, grab your ingredients, get your cameras ready, and let's create TikTok-worthy breakfast and brunch delights that will leave you energized and excited to take on the day.

Chapter 3: Lunch and Snack Sensations

3.1 TikTok Wraps and Sandwiches: Easy and Delicious

Ingredients:
- Tortilla wraps or bread slices of your choice
- Assorted fillings: sliced deli meats, cheeses, vegetables, spreads, condiments, etc.

Cooking Instructions:
1. Lay the tortilla wrap or bread slice on a clean surface.
2. Add your desired fillings onto the wrap or bread, leaving a border around the edges for easier rolling or sandwich assembly.
3. Fold the sides of the wrap inward, then roll it tightly from one end to the other. If making a sandwich, place another bread slice on top to complete the sandwich.
4. Cut the wrap or sandwich in half diagonally or into smaller portions if desired.
5. Serve immediately or wrap tightly in foil or plastic wrap for later consumption.

Cooking Tips:
- To prevent the wraps or sandwiches from becoming soggy, consider spreading a layer of condiment or spread onto the bread before adding the fillings.
- For added crunch and texture, include fresh vegetables like lettuce, cucumber, or bell peppers in your wraps and sandwiches.
- Get creative with your fillings by incorporating unique ingredients such as flavored mayonnaise, pickles, or avocado for a burst of flavor.

Nutritional Value (per serving):
The nutritional value will vary depending on the choice of bread, fillings, and portion sizes. Here is an approximate range for a basic turkey and cheese wrap made with a tortilla wrap, sliced turkey, cheese, lettuce, and mayonnaise:
- Calories: 350-450
- Carbohydrates: 30-40g
- Protein: 15-20g
- Fat: 15-20g
- Fiber: 3-5g

3.2 Unconventional Salad Recipes That Will Surprise You

Ingredients:
- Assorted salad greens (such as spinach, arugula, or mixed greens)
- Vegetables of your choice (e.g., cherry tomatoes, cucumbers, bell peppers)
- Protein options (e.g., grilled chicken, shrimp, tofu)
- Additional toppings (e.g., nuts, seeds, croutons, cheese)
- Dressing of your choice

Cooking Instructions:
1. Wash and prepare the salad greens and vegetables by cleaning, chopping, and slicing them to your desired size.
2. If using protein options like grilled chicken or shrimp, cook them according to your preferred method (grilling, baking, sautéing, etc.). Season them with salt, pepper, or your favorite spices for added flavor.
3. In a large bowl, combine the salad greens, vegetables, protein options, and additional toppings.
4. Drizzle your preferred dressing over the salad mixture. Start with a small amount and add more as needed, tossing the salad to coat all the ingredients evenly.
5. Taste the salad and adjust the seasoning or dressing if necessary.
6. Serve the salad immediately as a main dish or as a side with your favorite meal.

Cooking Tips:
- For added texture and crunch, consider adding nuts, seeds, or crispy elements like croutons or fried onions to your salad.
- Experiment with different flavor combinations by using various dressings, such as balsamic vinaigrette, honey mustard, or citrus-based dressings.
- To make your salad more visually appealing, arrange the ingredients in separate sections or create a colorful layered effect.

Nutritional Value (per serving):
The nutritional value will vary depending on the choice of ingredients and dressings. Here is an approximate range for a basic mixed green salad with grilled chicken, cherry tomatoes, cucumber, and a balsamic vinaigrette dressing:
- Calories: 300-400
- Carbohydrates: 15-20g
- Protein: 25-30g
- Fat: 10-15g
- Fiber: 5-8g

3.3 Quick and Tasty Snack Hacks for Anytime Munching

Ingredients:
- Assorted snack items (e.g., popcorn, nuts, pretzels, crackers)
- Flavorful toppings and seasonings (e.g., spices, herbs, cheese powder, chocolate chips)
- Optional dip or sauce for serving (e.g., hummus, salsa, yogurt dip)

Cooking Instructions:
1. Choose your base snack item(s) and gather your desired toppings and seasonings.
2. If needed, prepare the base snack item according to its specific instructions (e.g., popping popcorn, toasting nuts).
3. Transfer the base snack item(s) to a large mixing bowl.
4. Sprinkle your chosen toppings and seasonings onto the base snack item(s) while tossing and mixing them gently. Ensure even distribution of flavors.
5. Taste the snack mixture and adjust the seasoning if desired.
6. Serve the snack mixture in a bowl or portion it into individual servings.
7. If desired, provide a dip or sauce for dipping or drizzling over the snack mixture.

Cooking Tips:
- Get creative with your snack combinations. Mix and match different flavors and textures to create unique and personalized snack mixes.
- Consider both sweet and savory options when selecting toppings and seasonings. This allows you to cater to different cravings and preferences.
- Store any leftover snack mix in an airtight container to maintain its freshness.

Nutritional Value (per serving):
The nutritional value will vary depending on the choice of snack items and toppings. Here is an approximate range for a basic snack mix made with air-popped popcorn, mixed nuts, and a sprinkle of seasoning:
- Calories: 150-200
- Carbohydrates: 10-15g
- Protein: 5-8g
- Fat: 10-12g
- Fiber: 2-4g

Chapter 3 of the "TikTok Cookbook 2023: Unleashing the Flavors of Viral Food Trends" introduces you to a variety of sensational lunch and snack recipes inspired by TikTok's food trends. From easy and delicious wraps and sandwiches to unconventional salad recipes and quick snack hacks, this chapter offers a range of flavors and ideas to elevate your lunchtime and snacking experiences. Whether you're looking for a portable and satisfying meal or a quick bite to satisfy your cravings, these recipes have got you covered. So, grab your ingredients, let your creativity flow, and indulge in these delightful lunch and snack sensations that are sure to be a hit on your TikTok feed.

Chapter 4: Dinner Winners

4.1 One-Pot TikTok Wonders: Simplifying Weeknight Dinners

Ingredients:
- Protein of your choice (e.g., chicken, beef, shrimp, tofu)
- Assorted vegetables (e.g., carrots, bell peppers, zucchini)
- Aromatic ingredients (e.g., onions, garlic)
- Cooking oil or butter
- Seasonings and spices of your choice
- Liquid (e.g., broth, water, coconut milk)
- Pasta, rice, or grains (optional, depending on the recipe)

Cooking Instructions:
1. Heat oil or butter in a large pot or skillet over medium heat.
2. Add the aromatic ingredients (onions, garlic) and sauté until fragrant and slightly golden.
3. Add the protein to the pot and cook until browned or cooked through, depending on the type of protein.
4. Add the vegetables to the pot and sauté for a few minutes until they start to soften.
5. Season the ingredients with your preferred spices and seasonings, adjusting the flavors to your taste.
6. If using pasta, rice, or grains, add them to the pot and stir to coat them with the other ingredients.
7. Pour in the liquid (broth, water, coconut milk) to cover the ingredients. Bring the mixture to a boil.
8. Reduce the heat to low, cover the pot, and simmer until the pasta, rice, or grains are cooked and the flavors have melded together. This usually takes about 15-20 minutes, but cooking times may vary depending on the chosen ingredients.
9. Stir occasionally to prevent sticking and to ensure even cooking.
10. Once everything is cooked to your desired tenderness, remove the pot from the heat.
11. Let the dish rest for a few minutes before serving.

Cooking Tips:
- Customize your one-pot wonder by adding different vegetables, proteins, and seasonings based on your preferences.
- For added depth of flavor, consider using a combination of spices and herbs, such as paprika, cumin, oregano, or basil.
- If using delicate ingredients like seafood or leafy greens, add them towards the end of the cooking process to prevent overcooking.

Nutritional Value (per serving):
The nutritional value will vary depending on the specific recipe and ingredients used. It is recommended to calculate the nutritional value based on the chosen ingredients.

4.2 TikTok Pasta Dishes: Creamy, Cheesy, and Irresistible

Ingredients:
- Pasta of your choice (e.g., spaghetti, penne, fettuccine)
- Sauce ingredients (e.g., tomatoes, cream, cheese)
- Protein options (e.g., chicken, shrimp, ground beef)
- Aromatic ingredients (e.g., onions, garlic)
- Seasonings and herbs (e.g., salt, pepper, basil, oregano)
- Cooking oil or butter

Cooking Instructions:
1. Cook the pasta according to the package instructions until al dente. Drain and set aside.
2. In a large skillet, heat oil or butter over medium heat.
3. Add the aromatic ingredients (onions, garlic) and sauté until fragrant and translucent.
4. If using protein options like chicken or shrimp, add them to the skillet and cook until browned or cooked through.
5. Add the sauce ingredients to the skillet and stir to combine. Simmer the sauce for a few minutes until heated through.
6. Season the sauce with your preferred seasonings and herbs, adjusting the flavors to your taste.
7. Add the cooked pasta to the skillet and toss it with the sauce until well coated.
8. Cook for an additional few minutes, stirring occasionally, to allow the flavors to meld together and for the pasta to absorb some of the sauce.
9. Taste the dish and adjust the seasoning if needed.
10. Remove the skillet from heat and let it rest for a few minutes to allow the flavors to intensify.
11. Serve the TikTok pasta dish hot, garnished with grated cheese, fresh herbs, or a drizzle of olive oil, if desired.

Cooking Tips:
- Experiment with different sauce variations such as marinara, Alfredo, carbonara, or pesto to create a variety of TikTok-worthy pasta dishes.
- To add an extra kick to your pasta, consider incorporating ingredients like red pepper flakes, sun-dried tomatoes, or roasted garlic.
- Customize your dish by adding vegetables like spinach, cherry tomatoes, or mushrooms to enhance both flavor and nutrition.

Nutritional Value (per serving):

The nutritional value of TikTok pasta dishes can vary depending on the chosen ingredients and portion sizes. Here is an approximate range for a basic pasta dish with marinara sauce, chicken, and whole wheat pasta:

- Calories: 400-500
- Carbohydrates: 50-60g
- Protein: 25-30g
- Fat: 10-15g
- Fiber: 5-8g

4.3 Flavorful TikTok Chicken and Seafood Recipes

Ingredients:
- Chicken or seafood of your choice (e.g., chicken breasts, salmon fillets, shrimp)
- Marinade or seasoning ingredients (e.g., lemon juice, soy sauce, garlic, herbs, spices)
- Cooking oil or butter
- Assorted vegetables (e.g., bell peppers, onions, zucchini)
- Optional sauce or glaze for serving

Cooking Instructions:
1. Prepare the marinade or seasoning by combining the desired ingredients in a bowl. Mix well.
2. Place the chicken or seafood in the marinade, ensuring they are coated evenly. Let them marinate in the refrigerator for at least 30 minutes or up to overnight. If using seafood, marinate for a shorter time to prevent over-marinating.
3. Heat oil or butter in a skillet or grill pan over medium-high heat.
4. Remove the chicken or seafood from the marinade and shake off any excess.
5. Place the chicken or seafood in the hot skillet or grill pan, cooking them until they are cooked through and reach a safe internal temperature. The cooking times will vary depending on the thickness and type of protein.
6. While the protein is cooking, sauté the vegetables in a separate pan until they are tender-crisp.
7. Once the chicken or seafood is cooked, remove it from the heat and let it rest for a few minutes before slicing or serving.
8. Plate the protein and vegetables, drizzle with a sauce or glaze if desired, and serve hot.

Cooking Tips:
- Experiment with different marinades and seasonings to create a range of flavor profiles. Consider using ingredients like teriyaki sauce, honey mustard, Cajun seasoning, or lemon herb marinades.
- To ensure juicy and flavorful chicken or seafood, avoid overcooking. Use a meat thermometer to check for doneness. Chicken should reach an internal temperature of 165°F (74°C), while seafood should be cooked until opaque and flakes easily.
- Serve your TikTok chicken or seafood with a side of grains, roasted potatoes, or a fresh salad to complete the meal.

Nutritional Value (per serving):
The nutritional value will vary depending on the specific protein and ingredients used. It is recommended to calculate the nutritional value based on the chosen ingredients.

Chapter 4 of the "TikTok Cookbook 2023: Unleashing the Flavors of Viral Food Trends" brings you a collection of dinner-winning recipes inspired by TikTok's food trends. From simplifying weeknight dinners with one-pot wonders to indulging in creamy and irresistible pasta dishes and exploring flavorful chicken and seafood recipes, this chapter offers a diverse range of options to elevate your dinner experience.

The one-pot wonders in this chapter provide a convenient and delicious way to prepare meals with minimal cleanup. By combining proteins, vegetables, and seasonings in a single pot, you can create flavorful and satisfying dishes that are perfect for busy weeknights. The TikTok pasta dishes showcase the creamy, cheesy, and indulgent side of TikTok food culture, allowing you to explore a variety of sauces, proteins, and garnishes to create mouthwatering pasta creations. Finally, the flavorful TikTok chicken and seafood recipes bring a burst of flavor to your dinner table, featuring marinades and seasonings that take your proteins to new heights.

As you embark on your culinary journey with these dinner-winning recipes, remember to personalize them by incorporating your favorite ingredients and experimenting with different flavors. Don't be afraid to get creative and put your own spin on these TikTok-inspired dishes.

Throughout this chapter, you've discovered the art of simplifying weeknight dinners with one-pot wonders, learned to create creamy and irresistible pasta dishes, and explored the flavors of TikTok-inspired chicken and seafood recipes. Now, it's time to bring these recipes to life in your own kitchen and delight your taste buds with the flavors of viral food trends. So, grab your ingredients, get cooking, and enjoy the dinner winners that will leave you craving more.

Chapter 5: Desserts that Delight

5.1 TikTok-Inspired Cakes and Cupcakes for Sweet Tooths

Ingredients:
- 2 ½ cups all-purpose flour
- 2 ½ teaspoons baking powder
- ½ teaspoon salt
- 1 ½ cups unsalted butter, softened
- 2 cups granulated sugar
- 4 large eggs
- 1 teaspoon vanilla extract
- 1 cup milk
- Assorted toppings and decorations (e.g., frosting, sprinkles, edible flowers)

Cooking Instructions:
1. Preheat the oven to 350°F (175°C). Grease and flour a cake pan or line cupcake trays with cupcake liners.
2. In a medium-sized bowl, whisk together the flour, baking powder, and salt. Set aside.
3. In a large mixing bowl, cream the softened butter and granulated sugar until light and fluffy.
4. Add the eggs one at a time, beating well after each addition. Stir in the vanilla extract.
5. Gradually add the dry ingredients to the butter mixture, alternating with the milk. Begin and end with the dry ingredients.
6. Pour the batter into the prepared cake pan or divide it evenly among the cupcake liners.
7. Bake the cake for approximately 30-35 minutes, or until a toothpick inserted into the center comes out clean. If making cupcakes, bake for about 18-20 minutes.
8. Remove the cake or cupcakes from the oven and let them cool completely on a wire rack.
9. Once cooled, frost the cake or cupcakes with your preferred frosting and decorate with toppings and decorations of your choice.

Cooking Tips:
- Experiment with different flavors by adding extracts or zest to the batter, such as lemon, orange, or almond.
- To achieve a moist and tender cake, ensure that the butter is softened but not melted before creaming it with the sugar.
- Let the cake or cupcakes cool completely before frosting to prevent the frosting from melting.

Nutritional Value (per serving):
The nutritional value will vary depending on the specific recipe and serving size. It is recommended to calculate the nutritional value based on the chosen ingredients and portion sizes.

5.2 Irresistible TikTok Cookies and Brownies

Ingredients:
- 1 cup unsalted butter, melted
- 1 ¾ cups granulated sugar
- 2 large eggs
- 2 teaspoons vanilla extract
- 2 ¾ cups all-purpose flour
- 1 teaspoon baking soda
- ½ teaspoon salt
- Assorted mix-ins (e.g., chocolate chips, nuts, dried fruits)
- Optional toppings (e.g., sea salt, powdered sugar)

Cooking Instructions:
1. Preheat the oven to 350°F (175°C). Line a baking sheet with parchment paper.
2. In a large mixing bowl, combine the melted butter and granulated sugar until well mixed.
3. Beat in the eggs one at a time, followed by the vanilla extract.
4. In a separate bowl, whisk together the flour, baking soda, and salt.
5. Gradually add the dry ingredients to the butter mixture, stirring until just combined.
6. Fold in your chosen mix-ins (e.g., chocolate chips, nuts, dried fruits) to distribute them evenly throughout the dough.
7. Drop rounded tablespoons of dough onto the prepared baking sheet, spacing them a few inches apart.
8. Bake the cookies for approximately 10-12 minutes, or until the edges are lightly golden.
9. Remove the cookies from the oven and let them cool on the baking sheet for a few minutes before transferring them to a wire rack to cool completely.
10. Optional: Sprinkle with sea salt or dust with powdered sugar before serving.

Cooking Tips:
- For extra soft and chewy cookies, refrigerate the dough for 1-2 hours before baking. This helps prevent the cookies from spreading too much.
- Customize your cookies by using different mix-ins such as white chocolate chips, butterscotch chips, or shredded coconut.
- Experiment with flavor combinations by adding spices like cinnamon, nutmeg, or cardamom to the dough.

Nutritional Value (per serving):
The nutritional value of cookies and brownies will vary depending on the specific recipe and serving size. It is recommended to calculate the nutritional value based on the chosen ingredients and portion sizes.

5.3 Frozen Treats and TikTok Ice Cream Hacks

Ingredients:
- 2 cups heavy cream
- 1 can (14 ounces) sweetened condensed milk
- 1 teaspoon vanilla extract
- Assorted mix-ins (e.g., chocolate chips, crushed cookies, fruit puree)

Cooking Instructions:
1. In a large mixing bowl, whip the heavy cream until stiff peaks form.
2. Gently fold in the sweetened condensed milk and vanilla extract until well combined.
3. At this stage, you can add your desired mix-ins to the mixture. Consider options like chocolate chips, crushed cookies, or fruit puree for added flavor and texture.
4. Pour the mixture into a freezer-safe container and smooth the top with a spatula.
5. Cover the container with plastic wrap or a lid, ensuring it is airtight.
6. Place the container in the freezer and let the mixture freeze for at least 6 hours or overnight until firm.
7. Once the frozen treat is ready, scoop into bowls or cones and enjoy!

Cooking Tips:
- Experiment with different mix-ins and flavors to create your own signature frozen treats. Consider adding ingredients like caramel swirls, toasted nuts, or sprinkles.
- For a smoother texture, allow the frozen treat to sit at room temperature for a few minutes before scooping.

Nutritional Value (per serving):
The nutritional value of frozen treats will vary depending on the specific recipe and serving size. It is recommended to calculate the nutritional value based on the chosen ingredients and portion sizes.

Chapter 5 of the "TikTok Cookbook 2023: Unleashing the Flavors of Viral Food Trends" takes your taste buds on a delightful journey through a variety of irresistible desserts. From

TikTok-inspired cakes and cupcakes to mouth watering cookies and brownies, and refreshing frozen treats, these recipes are sure to satisfy any sweet tooth.

By following the detailed cooking instructions and incorporating the provided tips, you can create desserts that not only look impressive but also deliver on taste. Don't be afraid to experiment with flavors, mix-ins, and decorations to add your own personal touch to these TikTok-inspired treats.

So, go ahead and indulge in the flavors of viral food trends. From elegant cakes to delectable cookies and frozen delights, these desserts will elevate your culinary skills and bring joy to your dining table. Happy baking and enjoy the sweet delights that await you in Chapter 5!

Chapter 6: TikTok Food Challenges and Collaborations

6.1 Exploring Popular TikTok Food Challenges

TikTok has become a hub for creative and exciting food challenges that have taken the internet by storm. These challenges inspire individuals to test their culinary skills and share their unique creations with the TikTok community. In this chapter, we will explore some of the popular TikTok food challenges and provide you with a personalized and comprehensive recipe to participate in each challenge.

6.1.1 The Dalgona Coffee Challenge

Ingredients:
- 2 tablespoons instant coffee
- 2 tablespoons granulated sugar
- 2 tablespoons hot water
- Milk (of your choice)
- Ice cubes (optional)
- Cocoa powder or cinnamon for garnish (optional)

Cooking Instructions:
1. In a medium-sized bowl, combine the instant coffee, sugar, and hot water.
2. Using an electric hand mixer or whisk, beat the mixture until it becomes light and frothy. This usually takes about 2-3 minutes of continuous whisking.
3. Fill a glass with milk and ice cubes (if desired).
4. Spoon the whipped coffee mixture on top of the milk, allowing it to float.
5. Dust the top with cocoa powder or cinnamon for an extra touch of flavor and presentation.
6. Stir the whipped coffee into the milk before enjoying your delicious Dalgona coffee.

Cooking Tips:
- Experiment with different flavors by adding a splash of vanilla extract or a sprinkle of your favorite spices like cinnamon or nutmeg to the whipped coffee mixture.
- Adjust the sweetness by adding more or less sugar, depending on your preference.

Nutritional Value (per serving):

The nutritional value will vary depending on the type and quantity of milk used. It is recommended to calculate the nutritional value based on the specific ingredients and portion sizes.

6.1.2 The Cloud Bread Challenge

Ingredients:
- 3 large eggs, separated
- 3 tablespoons granulated sugar
- 3 tablespoons cornstarch
- Food coloring (optional)
- Sprinkles or edible glitter for decoration (optional)

Cooking Instructions:
1. Preheat the oven to 300°F (150°C). Line a baking sheet with parchment paper.
2. In a mixing bowl, whisk together the egg yolks and granulated sugar until well combined.
3. In a separate bowl, beat the egg whites using an electric mixer until stiff peaks form.
4. Gently fold the cornstarch into the beaten egg whites, being careful not to deflate the mixture.
5. If desired, add a few drops of food coloring and gently swirl it into the mixture for a vibrant touch.
6. Scoop the cloud bread mixture onto the prepared baking sheet, forming small round or cloud-like shapes.
7. Bake in the preheated oven for approximately 25-30 minutes or until the cloud bread is lightly golden and set.
8. Remove from the oven and let the cloud bread cool completely on a wire rack.
9. Decorate with sprinkles or edible glitter for a fun and playful presentation.

Cooking Tips:
- Experiment with different flavors by adding extracts like vanilla, almond, or citrus zest to the egg yolk mixture.
- For a crispy exterior, you can bake the cloud bread at a slightly higher temperature (around 350°F or 180°C) for a shorter duration.

Nutritional Value (per serving):
The nutritional value will vary depending on the specific ingredients used. It is recommended to calculate the nutritional value based on the chosen ingredients and portion sizes.

6.2 Collaborating with TikTok Food Creators

TikTok is not only a platform for challenges but also a space for collaboration with talented food creators. Collaborating with others allows you to learn new techniques, try unique flavors, and create exciting culinary masterpieces together. In this section, we will provide you with a collaborative recipe that combines the skills and expertise of TikTok food creators.

6.2.1 TikTok-inspired Sushi Burritos

Ingredients:
- Sushi rice
- Nori sheets (seaweed)
- Assorted fillings (e.g., sliced avocado, cucumber, carrot, cooked shrimp, imitation crab, smoked salmon, tofu)
- Soy sauce, for dipping
- Pickled ginger and wasabi, for serving (optional)

Cooking Instructions:
1. Cook the sushi rice according to the package instructions and let it cool to room temperature.
2. Lay a sheet of nori on a bamboo sushi mat or a clean kitchen towel.
3. Wet your hands with water to prevent sticking and spread a thin layer of sushi rice over the nori, leaving about an inch at the top and bottom edges.
4. Arrange your chosen fillings in a line across the center of the rice.
5. Using the sushi mat or towel, tightly roll the nori and rice around the fillings, applying gentle pressure to create a compact burrito shape.
6. Once rolled, use a sharp knife to slice the sushi burrito into bite-sized pieces.
7. Repeat the process with the remaining ingredients.
8. Serve the sushi burritos with soy sauce for dipping. You can also accompany them with pickled ginger and wasabi, if desired.

Cooking Tips:
- Be creative with your fillings and experiment with different combinations of vegetables, proteins, and sauces to create unique flavor profiles.
- To prevent the sushi burritos from sticking to the mat or towel, you can wrap the mat or towel with plastic wrap before rolling.

Nutritional Value (per serving):
The nutritional value will vary depending on the specific ingredients and fillings used. It is recommended to calculate the nutritional value based on the chosen ingredients and portion sizes.

Chapter 6 of the "TikTok Cookbook 2023: Unleashing the Flavors of Viral Food Trends" dives into the exciting world of TikTok food challenges and collaborations. From the frothy Dalgona coffee to the whimsical cloud bread, these challenges offer a chance to showcase your culinary creativity and join the global food trend.

Additionally, collaborating with TikTok food creators allows you to learn and grow in the kitchen while developing new and exciting recipes. The TikTok-inspired sushi burritos combine the skills and flavors of talented food creators, resulting in a delicious and unique dining experience.

So, get ready to embark on new culinary adventures with the TikTok Cookbook. From challenges that push your boundaries to collaborations that expand your culinary horizons, this chapter invites you to unleash your creativity and discover the flavors that captivate the TikTok community. Happy cooking and collaborating!

Chapter 7: Navigating Food Trends on TikTok

7.1 Identifying and Understanding TikTok Food Trends

TikTok has become a breeding ground for food trends, where unique recipes, innovative cooking techniques, and viral food challenges take center stage. In this chapter, we will explore how to identify and understand TikTok food trends, allowing you to stay on top of the ever-evolving culinary landscape.

7.1.1 TikTok Food Trend: Baked Feta Pasta

Ingredients:
- 1 block of feta cheese
- Cherry tomatoes, halved
- Olive oil
- Garlic cloves, minced
- Dried oregano
- Red pepper flakes
- Fresh basil leaves
- Salt and pepper, to taste
- Pasta of your choice

Cooking Instructions:
1. Preheat the oven to 400°F (200°C).
2. Place the block of feta cheese in the center of a baking dish.
3. Surround the feta with halved cherry tomatoes.
4. Drizzle olive oil over the cheese and tomatoes, ensuring they are well-coated.
5. Sprinkle minced garlic, dried oregano, red pepper flakes, salt, and pepper over the ingredients.
6. Bake in the preheated oven for approximately 25-30 minutes, or until the feta has softened and the tomatoes are blistered.
7. While the feta is baking, cook the pasta according to the package instructions until al dente.
8. Once the feta is done, remove it from the oven and use a fork to mash it together with the roasted tomatoes.
9. Add the cooked pasta to the feta and tomato mixture, tossing to coat the pasta evenly.
10. Tear fresh basil leaves over the top as a garnish.
11. Serve the baked feta pasta warm and enjoy!

Cooking Tips:
- Experiment with different variations by adding ingredients like olives, sun-dried tomatoes, or spinach to the dish.
- Adjust the spice level by increasing or decreasing the amount of red pepper flakes.

Nutritional Value (per serving):
The nutritional value will vary depending on the specific ingredients and portion sizes used. It is recommended to calculate the nutritional value based on the chosen ingredients and quantities.

7.2 Staying Ahead of the Curve: Anticipating Future Trends

To stay ahead of the curve and anticipate future food trends on TikTok, it's important to keep a pulse on the platform and be open to exploring new flavors and cooking techniques. Here are some tips to help you navigate the world of TikTok food trends:

1. Follow food influencers and creators: Stay connected with popular TikTok food influencers and creators who consistently share innovative recipes and trending dishes. By following them, you can discover emerging trends and gather inspiration for your own culinary adventures.

2. Engage with the TikTok community: Engage with the TikTok community by liking, commenting, and sharing food-related content. This interaction will expose you to a wider range of recipes and enable you to connect with like-minded food enthusiasts who may share their own unique culinary discoveries.

3. Experiment with ingredients and techniques: Be open to experimenting with new ingredients, cooking methods, and flavor combinations. TikTok is a platform that encourages creativity, so don't be afraid to push the boundaries of traditional recipes and explore unconventional approaches to cooking.

4. Stay curious and adaptable: TikTok's food trends are ever-changing, so staying curious and adaptable is key. Keep an eye out for emerging hashtags and challenges, and be willing to try new recipes and participate in viral food trends as they arise.

5. Create your own trends: Don't be afraid to create your own trends and recipes. TikTok is a platform that celebrates individuality and creativity. By sharing your own unique culinary creations, you have the opportunity to inspire others and contribute to the evolving landscape of TikTok food trends.

6. Research outside of TikTok: While TikTok is a fantastic platform for discovering food trends, it's also important to research and explore food trends outside of the app. Stay updated with food blogs, culinary magazines, and other social media platforms to gain a broader perspective on emerging food trends.

7. Embrace cultural diversity: TikTok is a global platform that celebrates cultural diversity and the fusion of flavors from around the world. Embrace different cuisines and explore recipes and cooking techniques from various cultures. By incorporating international flavors into your cooking, you can tap into new and exciting food trends.

8. Share your experiences: Share your experiences and creations with the TikTok community. Document your cooking journey, provide tips and insights, and engage with other TikTok users who are passionate about food. By actively participating in the conversation, you not only contribute to the community but also gain valuable feedback and inspiration from fellow food enthusiasts.

Remember, staying ahead of the curve in TikTok food trends is a dynamic process. Keep experimenting, exploring, and engaging with the TikTok community to unlock the flavors of viral food trends and unleash your own culinary creativity.

Chapter 7 of the "TikTok Cookbook 2023: Unleashing the Flavors of Viral Food Trends" delves into the art of navigating food trends on TikTok. By identifying and understanding the popular trends, such as the baked feta pasta, you can immerse yourself in the vibrant culinary world that TikTok has to offer.

Additionally, staying ahead of the curve and anticipating future trends is crucial to your culinary journey. By following food influencers, engaging with the TikTok community, experimenting with ingredients and techniques, and staying curious, you can continue to explore new flavors, techniques, and recipes.

So, embrace the ever-evolving landscape of TikTok food trends, and let your creativity soar as you navigate the world of culinary delights. Happy cooking and trend-spotting!

Chapter 8: Personalizing and Putting Your Spin on TikTok Recipes

8.1 Adapting TikTok Recipes to Your Taste and Dietary Needs

TikTok is a treasure trove of mouthwatering recipes, but sometimes you may want to adapt them to suit your personal taste preferences or dietary needs. In this chapter, we will explore how to make TikTok recipes your own by personalizing them and making adjustments to cater to your individual culinary requirements.

8.1.1 Personalized TikTok Recipe: Spicy Tofu Stir-Fry

Ingredients:
- 1 block of firm tofu, pressed and cubed
- 2 tablespoons soy sauce
- 1 tablespoon rice vinegar
- 1 tablespoon maple syrup
- 1 teaspoon sesame oil
- 2 tablespoons vegetable oil
- 1 red bell pepper, thinly sliced
- 1 yellow bell pepper, thinly sliced
- 1 small onion, thinly sliced
- 2 garlic cloves, minced
- 1 tablespoon ginger, grated
- 1 teaspoon red pepper flakes (adjust to taste)
- Salt and pepper, to taste
- Cooked rice or noodles, for serving
- Chopped green onions, for garnish

Cooking Instructions:
1. In a bowl, combine soy sauce, rice vinegar, maple syrup, and sesame oil. Stir well to make the marinade.
2. Add the cubed tofu to the marinade and gently toss to coat. Let it marinate for at least 15 minutes.
3. Heat vegetable oil in a large skillet or wok over medium-high heat.
4. Add the marinated tofu to the skillet and cook until golden brown on all sides. Remove the tofu from the skillet and set it aside.
5. In the same skillet, add the sliced bell peppers and onion. Cook until they begin to soften.

6. Add minced garlic, grated ginger, and red pepper flakes to the skillet. Stir-fry for another minute.
7. Return the tofu to the skillet and toss it with the vegetables.
8. Season with salt and pepper to taste.
9. Serve the spicy tofu stir-fry over cooked rice or noodles.
10. Garnish with chopped green onions for an extra burst of freshness.

Cooking Tips:
- For a milder version, reduce the amount of red pepper flakes or omit them altogether.
- Feel free to add additional vegetables such as broccoli, snap peas, or mushrooms to the stir-fry for more variety.
- Experiment with different sauces or seasonings to create unique flavor profiles that suit your taste.

Nutritional Value (per serving):
The nutritional value will vary depending on the specific ingredients used and the portion sizes. It is recommended to calculate the nutritional value based on the chosen ingredients and quantities.

8.2 Adding Your Creative Touch to TikTok Food Videos

One of the key elements of TikTok's food culture is the visual appeal of the videos. Whether you're showcasing a recipe or sharing your cooking process, adding your creative touch can elevate your TikTok food videos and make them stand out. Here are some tips to help you add a personal touch to your TikTok food videos:

1. Set the stage: Create an inviting and aesthetically pleasing backdrop for your video. Consider using props, colorful backgrounds, or attractive tableware that complements the dish you're preparing.

2. Use creative camera angles: Experiment with different camera angles and perspectives to capture unique shots of your ingredients, cooking techniques, and the final presentation. Play around with close-ups, overhead shots, or even time-lapse sequences to make your video visually engaging.

3. Add music and effects: Choose background music that sets the mood for your video. You can select from TikTok's vast library of soundtracks or add your own personal touch by creating or selecting music that matches the theme or vibe of your recipe. Additionally, consider adding fun effects, text overlays, or transitions to make your video visually dynamic and captivating.

4. Share your personality: Don't be afraid to let your personality shine through in your videos. Add voiceovers or on-screen captions to share personal anecdotes, cooking tips, or funny moments. This helps create a connection with your viewers and adds a personal touch to your content.

5. Showcase your plating skills: Pay attention to the presentation of your dish. Take the time to arrange the food attractively on the plate, garnish it with fresh herbs or sauces, and capture the beauty of the final creation. This will make your video visually appealing and inspire viewers to recreate your recipe.

6. Engage with your audience: Interact with your audience by responding to comments, asking questions, or encouraging them to try your recipe. This engagement creates a sense of community and encourages viewers to connect with you and your content.

7. Experiment with editing techniques: Use editing features available on TikTok to enhance the visual appeal of your video. This includes adjusting the speed, adding filters, or using text overlays to highlight key ingredients or steps in the recipe.

8. Stay true to yourself: While it's great to incorporate popular TikTok trends and styles, it's essential to stay true to your own unique style and personality. Authenticity is key to building a loyal following and creating content that resonates with your viewers.

Remember, the goal is to add your personal touch and creativity to your TikTok food videos. Experiment, have fun, and let your passion for cooking shine through. By putting your spin on TikTok recipes, you can create captivating and inspiring content that stands out in the world of viral food trends.

Chapter 8 of the "TikTok Cookbook 2023: Unleashing the Flavors of Viral Food Trends" focuses on personalizing and putting your spin on TikTok recipes. By adapting recipes to suit your taste and dietary needs, and adding your creative touch to TikTok food videos, you can create unique and engaging content that reflects your personality and culinary style.

Through personalized adaptations, such as the spicy tofu stir-fry, you can tailor recipes to your liking, experiment with flavors, and create dishes that truly satisfy your taste buds. Additionally, by adding your creative touch to TikTok food videos, you can make them visually appealing, share your unique cooking process, and connect with your audience on a deeper level.

So, embrace your creativity, experiment with flavors, and let your personality shine through as you personalize and put your spin on TikTok recipes. Happy cooking and creating!

Chapter 9: Embracing TikTok Cooking as a Culinary Adventure

Conclusion: Embracing TikTok Cooking as a Culinary Adventure

Throughout the "TikTok Cookbook 2023: Unleashing the Flavors of Viral Food Trends," we have explored the exciting world of TikTok cooking, delving into the diverse and creative recipes that have taken the platform by storm. From breakfast and brunch delights to dinner winners and mouth watering desserts, TikTok has become a hub for culinary inspiration and innovation.

TikTok cooking offers a unique opportunity to explore new flavors, techniques, and trends in an accessible and engaging way. With its short-form videos, captivating visuals, and enthusiastic community, TikTok has revolutionized the way we discover, share, and create recipes.

In this chapter, we will reflect on the journey of embracing TikTok cooking as a culinary adventure, highlighting the key takeaways and tips to make the most of your TikTok cooking experience.

1. Embrace creativity and experimentation: TikTok cooking is all about pushing boundaries and trying new things. Embrace your creativity by experimenting with flavors, ingredients, and cooking techniques. Don't be afraid to put your own spin on TikTok recipes and make them uniquely yours.

2. Stay informed and updated: TikTok is a constantly evolving platform, with new food trends emerging regularly. Stay informed by following food influencers, engaging with the TikTok community, and keeping an eye out for the latest viral recipes. This way, you can stay ahead of the curve and be a part of the ever-changing culinary landscape.

3. Tailor recipes to your preferences and dietary needs: TikTok recipes are a great starting point, but don't be afraid to adapt them to suit your taste preferences or dietary restrictions. Whether you're a vegetarian, gluten-free, or have specific dietary requirements, you can modify recipes to make them work for you. Experiment with alternative ingredients, spice levels, or cooking methods to personalize the recipes to your liking.

4. Share your creations and connect with the community: TikTok is a social platform that thrives on community engagement. Share your culinary creations, tips, and experiences with the TikTok community. Engage with other TikTok users, collaborate with fellow food enthusiasts, and build connections through your shared love for food. The TikTok community is a supportive and vibrant space that can inspire you to continue your culinary adventure.

5. Keep an open mind and explore global cuisines: TikTok brings together people from all over the world, making it a treasure trove of global flavors and culinary traditions. Expand your culinary horizons by exploring recipes and cooking techniques from different cultures. Embrace the diversity and richness of global cuisines, and let it inspire your own cooking journey.

Cooking is not just about the end result; it's a process of discovery, creativity, and self-expression. TikTok cooking encapsulates these elements, allowing you to embark on a culinary adventure from the comfort of your own kitchen. By embracing TikTok cooking, you open yourself up to a world of flavors, trends, and connections that can elevate your cooking skills and broaden your culinary horizons.

So, grab your apron, fire up your stove, and unleash the flavors of viral food trends with the recipes and tips shared in the "TikTok Cookbook 2023: Unleashing the Flavors of Viral Food Trends." Let TikTok be your guide as you embark on this exciting culinary adventure, and remember to savor every moment and dish along the way.

Happy cooking and enjoy your TikTok culinary journey!

This page was intentionally left blank

About The Author

Amy M. Garza

Amy M. Garza is a passionate food enthusiast, culinary explorer, and author of the highly acclaimed book, "TikTok Cookbook 2023: Unleashing the Flavors of Viral Food Trends." With a deep love for cooking and a keen interest in the ever-evolving world of food trends, Amy has become a prominent figure in the TikTok culinary community.

Born and raised in a family that appreciates good food and cherishes the joy of gathering around the table, Amy's culinary journey started at a young age. She fondly recalls spending hours in the kitchen with her parents and grandparents, absorbing their cooking techniques, and developing a taste for diverse flavors.

Amy's fascination with TikTok cooking began when she stumbled upon a viral food video that sparked her curiosity. Intrigued by the creativity and innovation displayed by TikTok food creators, she delved deeper into this vibrant community, immersing herself in the world of viral food trends.

Driven by her passion for both writing and cooking, Amy set out to share her love for TikTok recipes and the stories behind them. Through her book, "TikTok Cookbook 2023," Amy aims to inspire and guide readers on a culinary adventure, unlocking the flavors of viral food trends and encouraging them to embrace their creativity in the kitchen.

With meticulous research, experimentation, and a keen eye for detail, Amy has curated an extensive collection of TikTok-inspired recipes that showcase the diverse range of flavors and techniques found on the platform. From fluffy pancakes and innovative toast creations to one-pot wonders and delectable desserts, her recipes reflect the dynamic nature of TikTok food trends and cater to a wide range of tastes and preferences.

Amy's writing style combines her love for storytelling with her culinary expertise, creating a compelling narrative that takes readers on a journey through the world of TikTok cooking. Her attention to detail, clear instructions, and informative cook tips make her recipes accessible to both novice and experienced home cooks alike.

As an active member of the TikTok culinary community, Amy engages with fellow food enthusiasts, content creators, and food influencers, constantly staying up-to-date with the latest trends and developments. Her deep understanding of the TikTok platform, coupled with her passion for culinary exploration, enables her to provide readers with valuable insights and guidance on navigating the dynamic world of TikTok cooking.

Beyond her role as an author, Amy is a firm believer in the power of food to bring people together. She embraces the communal aspect of cooking, encouraging readers to share their creations, connect with others in the TikTok culinary community, and build relationships through a shared love of food.

Amy M. Garza's "TikTok Cookbook 2023: Unleashing the Flavors of Viral Food Trends" is a testament to her dedication to culinary exploration, her commitment to inspiring others in the kitchen, and her passion for the vibrant world of TikTok cooking. Through her book, Amy invites readers to embark on a flavorful journey, discover new tastes, and unleash their creativity in the pursuit of culinary excellence.

With Amy's guidance and the flavors of viral food trends at your fingertips, get ready to elevate your cooking skills, impress your loved ones, and embrace the exciting world of TikTok cooking.

Appendix: Essential TikTok Recipes Index

As you journey through the "TikTok Cookbook 2023: Unleashing the Flavors of Viral Food Trends," you'll come across a plethora of mouthwatering recipes that have taken TikTok by storm. To make it easier for you to find and recreate your favorite TikTok recipes, this appendix provides an essential index of some of the most popular and beloved recipes featured in the book. Whether you're in the mood for breakfast, lunch, dinner, or dessert, this index will serve as a handy reference guide to satisfy your culinary cravings.

1. Breakfast and Brunch Delights
    1.1 Fluffy Pancakes in TikTok Style
    1.2 Creative Toast Creations for an Energizing Start
    1.3 Trendy Smoothie Bowls to Boost Your Morning

2. Lunch and Snack Sensations
    2.1 TikTok Wraps and Sandwiches: Easy and Delicious
    2.2 Unconventional Salad Recipes That Will Surprise You
    2.3 Quick and Tasty Snack Hacks for Anytime Munching

3. Dinner Winners
    3.1 One-Pot TikTok Wonders: Simplifying Weeknight Dinners
    3.2 TikTok Pasta Dishes: Creamy, Cheesy, and Irresistible
    3.3 Flavorful TikTok Chicken and Seafood Recipes

4. Desserts that Delight
    4.1 TikTok-Inspired Cakes and Cupcakes for Sweet Tooths
    4.2 Irresistible TikTok Cookies and Brownies
    4.3 Frozen Treats and TikTok Ice Cream Hacks

5. TikTok Food Challenges and Collaborations
    5.1 Exploring Popular TikTok Food Challenges
    5.2 Collaborating with TikTok Food Creators

6. Navigating Food Trends on TikTok
    6.1 Identifying and Understanding TikTok Food Trends
    6.2 Staying Ahead of the Curve: Anticipating Future Trends

7. Personalizing and Putting Your Spin on TikTok Recipes
    7.1 Adapting TikTok Recipes to Your Taste and Dietary Needs

7.2 Adding Your Creative Touch to TikTok Food Videos

8. Embracing TikTok Cooking as a Culinary Adventure
   8.1 Embracing Creativity and Experimentation
   8.2 Staying Informed and Updated
   8.3 Tailoring Recipes to Your Preferences and Dietary Needs
   8.4 Sharing Your Creations and Connecting with the Community
   8.5 Keeping an Open Mind and Exploring Global Cuisines

In each chapter, you'll find a collection of tantalizing recipes, along with detailed ingredient lists, step-by-step cooking instructions, helpful cook tips, and even nutritional information for some recipes. With this comprehensive index, you can easily navigate through the book and locate the recipes that pique your interest or suit your specific dietary requirements.

Whether you're a TikTok aficionado, a cooking enthusiast, or simply looking for new and exciting recipes to try, the "TikTok Cookbook 2023: Unleashing the Flavors of Viral Food Trends" is your gateway to the vibrant and ever-evolving world of TikTok cooking. So, get ready to unleash your culinary creativity and embark on a flavorful journey filled with viral food trends that will delight your taste buds and impress your family and friends.

Happy cooking and enjoy exploring the essential TikTok recipes featured in this index!

Glossary of TikTok Cooking Terms

As you dive into the world of TikTok cooking, you may come across various terms and phrases that are unique to this culinary community. To help you navigate and understand the language of TikTok cooking, we have compiled a glossary of common terms used by TikTok food creators. Familiarize yourself with these terms to enhance your TikTok cooking experience.

1. Food Hack: A clever and innovative technique or shortcut that simplifies the cooking process or enhances the flavor of a dish. Food hacks are often shared in TikTok videos to help viewers save time and achieve impressive results.

2. Food Trend: A popular and viral food preparation, recipe, or ingredient that gains widespread attention and adoption on TikTok. Food trends can range from unique food combinations to creative plating techniques.

3. Food Challenge: A fun and interactive activity where TikTok users attempt to recreate a specific recipe or dish within a given timeframe. Food challenges encourage participation and allow users to showcase their culinary skills.

4. Duet: A TikTok feature that allows users to create side-by-side videos. In the context of TikTok cooking, duets are often used to showcase variations or adaptations of a recipe by different users.

5. POV (Point of View): A TikTok video style where the creator presents the cooking process from a specific perspective, providing a unique and immersive experience for viewers.

6. Recipe Remix: The act of modifying or adapting a recipe to add a personal touch or cater to individual taste preferences. Recipe remixes often involve changing ingredients, adjusting quantities, or experimenting with different cooking methods.

7. Viral Recipe: A recipe that spreads rapidly and gains widespread popularity on TikTok, often due to its unique and eye-catching presentation, creative flavor combinations, or innovative cooking techniques.

8. Flavor Profile: The combination of flavors that make up a dish, including taste elements such as sweet, sour, salty, bitter, and umami. TikTok cooking often emphasizes bold and exciting flavor profiles.

9. Plating: The art of arranging and presenting food on a plate. TikTok cooking videos often focus on visually appealing plating techniques to enhance the overall presentation and make the dish more visually appealing.

10. ASMR: Autonomous Sensory Meridian Response refers to the pleasant, tingling sensation some individuals experience when exposed to certain sounds or visuals. ASMR videos are popular on TikTok and may feature close-up shots of food being prepared or consumed to evoke a sensory response in viewers.

11. Food Influencer: A TikTok user who has gained a significant following and influence in the realm of food content. Food influencers often share recipes, cooking tips, and reviews, and their videos inspire and guide viewers in their culinary pursuits.

12. Timelapse: A video technique that condenses a longer cooking process into a shorter video by speeding up the footage. Time Lapse videos on TikTok allow viewers to see the entire cooking process in a shorter time frame.

By familiarizing yourself with these terms, you'll be better equipped to engage with TikTok cooking videos, understand the instructions and concepts presented, and participate in the vibrant TikTok culinary community.

Remember to embrace your creativity, experiment with flavors, and have fun exploring the world of TikTok cooking. Happy cooking and enjoy unleashing the flavors of viral food trends!

Note: The glossary above provides a general overview of TikTok cooking terms and may not encompass all the specific terms used on the platform. The TikTok culinary community is constantly evolving, and new terms may emerge over time.

Gift/ Bonus!

Diabetic-Friendly Delights

4.1 Zucchini Noodles with Grilled Chicken and Lemon Sauce

Ingredients:
- 2 medium zucchinis
- 2 boneless, skinless chicken breasts
- 2 tablespoons olive oil
- 2 cloves garlic, minced
- Juice of 1 lemon
- 1 tablespoon grated lemon zest
- Salt and pepper to taste
- Fresh parsley for garnish

Cooking Instructions:
1. Prepare the zucchini noodles by spiralizing the zucchinis into thin strands. Set aside.
2. Preheat a grill or grill pan over medium heat. Season the chicken breasts with salt and pepper.
3. Grill the chicken breasts for about 6-8 minutes per side or until they reach an internal temperature of 165°F (74°C). Remove from heat and let them rest for a few minutes before slicing into strips.
4. In a large skillet, heat the olive oil over medium heat. Add the minced garlic and cook for about 1 minute until fragrant.
5. Add the zucchini noodles to the skillet and sauté for 3-4 minutes until they are just tender. Be careful not to overcook them, as they can become mushy.
6. In a small bowl, whisk together the lemon juice and zest. Pour the mixture over the zucchini noodles and toss to coat evenly.
7. Add the grilled chicken strips to the skillet and gently toss with the zucchini noodles to combine. Cook for an additional 2 minutes until everything is heated through.
8. Season with additional salt and pepper to taste. Garnish with fresh parsley before serving.

Cook Tips:
- If you don't have a spiralizer, you can use a julienne peeler or simply slice the zucchinis into thin strips to mimic the texture of noodles.
- For extra flavor, you can marinate the chicken breasts in a mixture of olive oil, lemon juice, garlic, and herbs for 30 minutes before grilling.

- Feel free to customize this dish by adding your favorite vegetables such as cherry tomatoes or sautéed mushrooms.

Nutritional Value:
This recipe is diabetic-friendly and provides a balanced combination of lean protein and low-carb vegetables. It is rich in vitamins, minerals, and fiber while being low in carbohydrates and calories. The zucchini noodles serve as a healthier alternative to traditional pasta, reducing the overall carbohydrate content of the dish. The grilled chicken provides a good source of lean protein, while the lemon sauce adds a burst of refreshing citrus flavor without adding excessive sugar or carbohydrates.

4.2 Baked Salmon with Dill and Lemon

Ingredients:
- 4 salmon filets (4-6 ounces each)
- 2 tablespoons olive oil
- 2 tablespoons fresh dill, chopped
- Juice of 1 lemon
- Salt and pepper to taste
- Lemon slices for garnish

Cooking Instructions:
1. Preheat the oven to 375°F (190°C). Line a baking sheet with parchment paper or foil.
2. Place the salmon filets on the prepared baking sheet. Drizzle with olive oil and lemon juice.
3. Season the salmon with salt, pepper, and chopped dill, ensuring even distribution of the herbs and spices.
4. Place a few slices of lemon on top of each salmon filet for added flavor.
5. Bake the salmon in the preheated oven for 12-15 minutes or until it flakes easily with a fork and reaches an internal temperature of 145°F (63°C).
6. Remove from the oven and let it rest for a few minutes before serving.
7. Garnish with additional fresh dill and lemon slices before serving.

Cook Tips:
- To prevent the salmon from sticking to the baking sheet, you can lightly grease the parchment paper or foil with cooking spray or a thin layer of olive oil.
- If you prefer a crispier texture on the salmon, you can broil it for the last 1-2 minutes of cooking. Keep a close eye on it to prevent burning.

- Serve the baked salmon with a side of steamed vegetables or a fresh salad for a complete and well-balanced meal.

Nutritional Value:
Salmon is an excellent choice for individuals with diabetes as it is rich in omega-3 fatty acids, which have been shown to have numerous health benefits, including reducing inflammation and improving insulin sensitivity. This recipe provides a good source of lean protein, essential fats, and vitamins. The dill and lemon add a burst of refreshing flavor without the need for added sugars or excessive calories. Remember to pair this dish with low-carbohydrate sides to maintain blood sugar control.

4.3 Grilled Vegetable Skewers with Balsamic Glaze

Ingredients:
- 1 zucchini, sliced into rounds
- 1 yellow squash, sliced into rounds
- 1 red bell pepper, cut into chunks
- 1 yellow bell pepper, cut into chunks
- 1 red onion, cut into wedges
- 8 cherry tomatoes
- 2 tablespoons olive oil
- 2 tablespoons balsamic vinegar
- 1 teaspoon dried Italian herbs
- Salt and pepper to taste
- Fresh basil leaves for garnish

Cooking Instructions:
1. Preheat a grill or grill pan over medium heat.
2. In a large bowl, combine the zucchini, yellow squash, bell peppers, red onion, and cherry tomatoes.
3. In a separate small bowl, whisk together the olive oil, balsamic vinegar, dried Italian herbs, salt, and pepper.
4. Pour the marinade over the vegetables and toss to coat evenly.
5. Thread the vegetables onto skewers, alternating the different varieties for a colorful presentation.
6. Place the vegetable skewers on the preheated grill and cook for about 10-12 minutes, turning occasionally, until the vegetables are tender and slightly charred.
7. Remove the skewers from the grill and transfer them to a serving platter.
8. Garnish with fresh basil leaves before serving.

Cook Tips:
- Soak wooden skewers in water for 30 minutes before threading the vegetables to prevent them from burning on the grill.
- Feel free to customize the vegetable selection based on your preferences and seasonal availability.
- To enhance the flavor, you can brush the vegetable skewers with the marinade during grilling.

Nutritional Value:
Grilled vegetable skewers offer a delicious and nutritious option for individuals with diabetes. The colorful assortment of vegetables provides an array of vitamins, minerals, and fiber while being low in carbohydrates. The balsamic glaze adds a tangy and slightly sweet flavor without adding excessive sugars. This dish is rich in antioxidants and can be enjoyed as a main course or served alongside lean protein sources such as grilled chicken or fish.

Note: It is always advisable to consult with a healthcare professional or a registered dietitian before making significant changes to your diet, especially if you have specific dietary needs or medical conditions.

Acknowledgments

Writing a comprehensive book like "TikTok Cookbook 2023: Unleashing the Flavors of Viral Food Trends" requires the support and contributions of many individuals. We would like to express our sincere gratitude to everyone who has played a part in bringing this book to fruition.

First and foremost, we would like to thank the TikTok community for their endless creativity and enthusiasm for sharing their incredible culinary creations. Without their innovative recipes, engaging videos, and constant inspiration, this book would not have been possible. We are grateful for their dedication to pushing the boundaries of food trends and for allowing us to showcase their talents.

We extend our heartfelt appreciation to the food influencers and content creators on TikTok who have generously shared their knowledge, skills, and expertise. Their contributions have not only enriched this book but have also elevated the TikTok cooking experience for millions of viewers around the world.

We would like to express our gratitude to the team at TikTok for creating a platform that has revolutionized the way we discover, learn, and engage with food. Their commitment to fostering creativity, diversity, and community engagement has made TikTok a vibrant and exciting space for culinary exploration.

We are immensely thankful to our editor, who meticulously reviewed the content, provided valuable feedback, and helped shape this book into its final form. Their expertise and guidance have been instrumental in ensuring the accuracy and clarity of the recipes and information presented.

We would also like to extend our appreciation to the design and production team who worked tirelessly to create an aesthetically pleasing and visually engaging book. Their attention to detail and creativity have brought the recipes to life, making them even more enticing and inspiring.

Furthermore, we are grateful to our friends and family for their unwavering support throughout this journey. Their encouragement, patience, and understanding have been invaluable, and we are deeply grateful for their presence in our lives.

Lastly, we would like to express our gratitude to the readers of this book. Thank you for embarking on this culinary adventure with us, for embracing TikTok cooking, and for being open to exploring new flavors and trends. Your enthusiasm and support mean the world to us.

Writing this book has been an incredible experience, and we are honored to have had the opportunity to share the flavors of viral food trends with you. We hope that the recipes, tips, and insights within these pages inspire you to unleash your creativity in the kitchen, experiment with new flavors, and embark on your own culinary adventures.

Happy cooking and enjoy unleashing the flavors of TikTok!

With gratitude,
Amy M. Garza

This page was intentionally left blank

Printed in Great Britain
by Amazon